ANIMAL NONSENSE RHYMES

When there's a fire in the jungle,
They call the Elephant Brigade,
Who race with their trunks full of water,
To the place that has to be sprayed,
But if the fire is a big one,
It happens as often as not,
That the elephants drink all the water,
To stop themselves getting too hot.

It's not only elephants who do the
unexpected in this hilarious A–Z of
animal rhymes! A host of quirky, zany
creatures frolic through its pages and
each rhyme is wittily complemented by
the author's own illustrations.

About the author

Born in 1943 in Hereford, Martin
Honeysett has had quite a varied career
since leaving art school. He worked in
Canada and New Zealand for several
years, doing a number of different jobs,
before returning to England in 1969 to
work as a bus driver for London
Transport; at the same time he began
drawing cartoons on a part-time basis.

He became a full-time freelance in 1972
and has since contributed cartoons
regularly to various well known
publications including *Punch*, *Private
Eye* and *Radio Times*. He has also
produced a number of cartoon books and
this is his first children's book.

He is married with two children.

ANIMAL NONSENSE RHYMES

MARTIN HONEYSETT

KNIGHT BOOKS
Hodder and Stoughton

Copyright © 1984 Martin Honeysett
First published in Great Britain 1984 by
Methuen Children's Books Ltd.

First published in Knight Books 1986

British Library C.I.P.

Honeysett, Martin
    Animal nonsense rhymes.
    I. Title
    821'.914   PR6058.052/

    ISBN 0–340–37241–9

Printed and bound in Great Britain for
Hodder and Stoughton Paperbacks, a
division of Hodder and Stoughton Ltd.,
Mill Road, Dunton Green, Sevenoaks,
Kent (Editorial Office: 47 Bedford
Square, London, WC1B 3DP) by
Cox & Wyman Ltd., Cardiff Road, Reading

Arnold was an Anteater,
He'd eat ants all day long,
"Eat lots of ants", his mother said,
"And you'll grow big and strong."
He had them fried for breakfast,
He had them stewed for lunch,
For tea he had them toasted,
They made a lovely crunch.
Alas, he liked to eat so much,
The poor lad couldn't stop,
He grew to a gigantic size,
And then one day went POP!

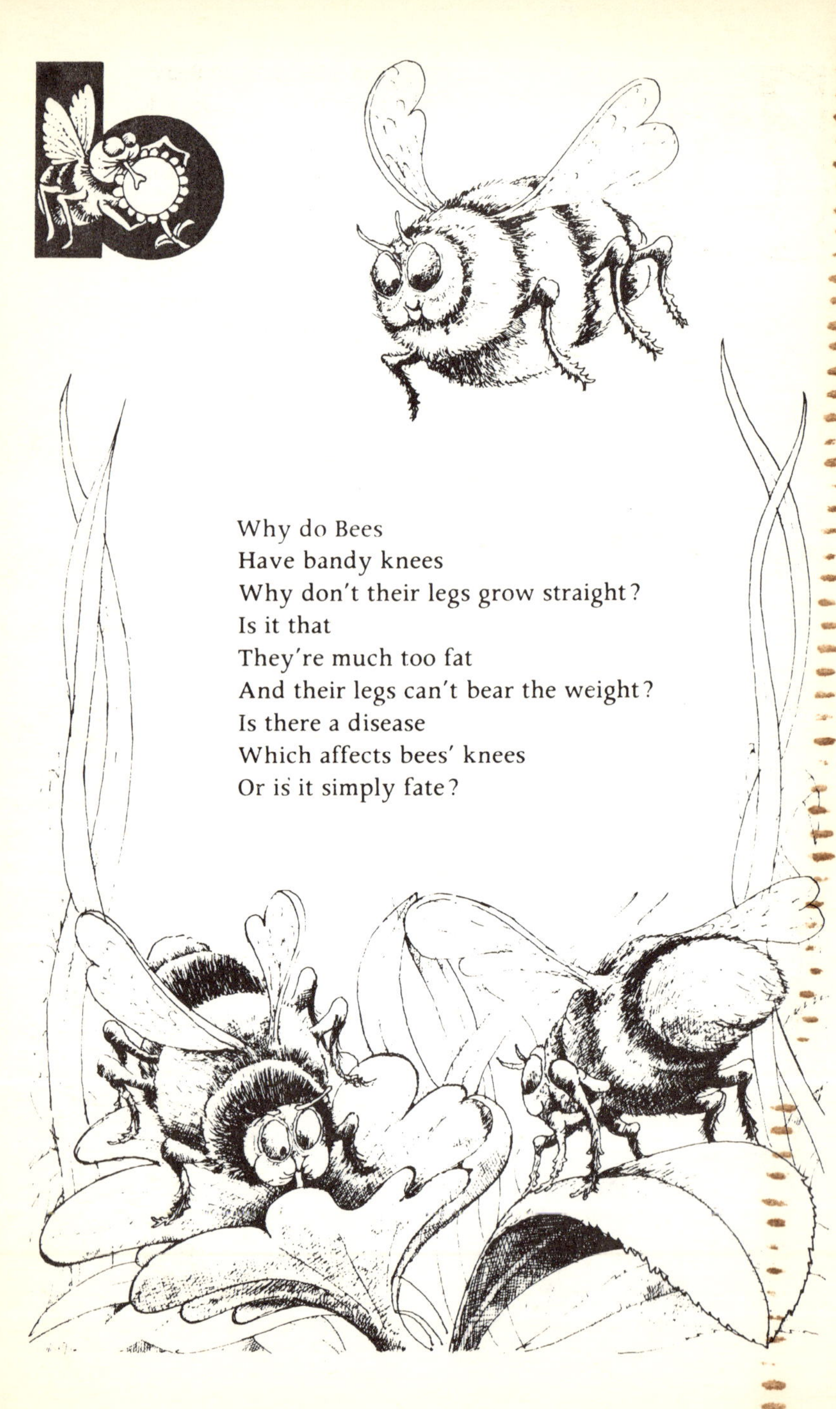

Why do Bees
Have bandy knees
Why don't their legs grow straight?
Is it that
They're much too fat
And their legs can't bear the weight?
Is there a disease
Which affects bees' knees
Or is it simply fate?

I'm a busy little Beaver,
I make things out of logs,
Not only dams but other things,
Like fencing posts and clogs.
I can gnaw you up
Some garden gates,
Or shelves on which
To stack your plates,
And if trade gets
A little poor,
I sell clothes pegs
From door to door.
But because I've been so busy,
I've worn out all my teeth,
And I haven't any more,
Growing up from underneath.
I tried to work without them,
But it made my gums so raw,
That now I do my woodwork,
With a little power saw.

Young Barney Bull felt rather sad,
He couldn't get angry like his dad,
His dad would stamp and bellow and roar,
And when he went out he'd slam the door.

But it hurt Barney's feet to stamp on the ground,
And his loudest bellow made hardly a sound,
His horns were bent and rather short,
And his nose would run if he tried to snort.

"I've decided," his father said one day,
"That Barney will have to be sent away,
There's a special school that I've been and seen,
Where they teach young bulls to be fierce and mean."

Barney left home with lots of tears,
Afraid he'd be gone for years and years,
But his work at the school was awfully good,
He learnt to get angry like all bulls should.

The exams, he passed without any bother,
And soon he was home with his father and mother,
Now, thanks to his parents' helping hand,
He's the angriest bull in all the land.

Mrs. Crocodile said to her daughter,
   "Now what would you like to be?
Have you thought what you'd like to do,
   When you're grown up like me?"

"Maybe a model," her daughter replied,
   "Though I'd have to be a bit slimmer,
Perhaps an airline stewardess,
   Or even a long distance swimmer."

"Well I never!" her mother exclaimed,
   "You've so many things to choose,
When I was a girl there was only one choice,
   You became either handbags or shoes."

The Centipedes in my garden
  Are such noisy little brutes,
I wish that they'd wear slippers
  Instead of hobnail boots.

I wish I had a Dolphin,
    It would make a smashing pet,
Maybe I could catch one,
    With my little fishing net.

I'd keep it in the bath at home,
    Though mother's bound to say,
"Get that great thing out at once,
    I've cleaned the bath today."

I'd take it to the swimming pool
    And ride upon its back.
I'd have to sneak it past the gate
    In a shopping bag or sack.

A Dolphin can be very smart,
    So I'd teach it lots of things,
To balance balls upon its head,
    And leap up high through rings.

But I only have a goldfish,
    And he can't leap at all,
He just lies there in his goldfish bowl
    Staring at the wall.

When there's a fire in the jungle,
They call the Elephant Brigade,
Who race with their trunks full of water,
To the place that has to be sprayed,
But if the fire is a big one,
It happens as often as not,
That the elephants drink all the water,
To stop themselves getting too hot.

EL

At jumping, Fernando the Frog was good,
He jumped much further than other frogs could.

In the morning when he jumped out of bed,
He would hit the ceiling with his head.

Fernando could jump the pond in one hop,
While the others got halfway and went plop.

But all that jumping made him so thin,
That one day he jumped right out of his skin.

He didn't jump much at all after that,
But just sat around and got rather fat.

If you see a frog who's tubby and bare,
It's poor Fernando with no skin to wear.

A giant Gorilla came to tea,
Whoever asked him? It wasn't me.
He came in through the kitchen wall,
It took six chairs to seat him all.
He drank his tea straight from the pot,
And sandwiches – he ate the lot.
He poked the jellies to make them wobble,
Then swallowed them up with just one gobble.
All that remained on the plate was the cake,
There was nothing else for him to take.
When he'd eaten that I showed him the door,
And hoped he'd go now there was no more.
Instead he ate the door as well,
Except for the knocker and the bell.
After that he at last decided to go,
Who invited him? I'd like to know.

Herby the Hippo wouldn't wallow in the mud,
Like his sister Ethel and his brother Bud.
"Do as you're told," his parents said,
"Or you'll have no supper and go straight to bed."

But day after day and week after week,
Herby refused to get in the creek.
His father got angry, his mother just sighed,
"You'll never get dirty like us," they cried.

Herby got so clean that he started to smell,
Which made the animals angry as well.
They said, "There's only one thing to do,
We'll send the young rascal away to a zoo."

So if you're at a zoo with a pong in the air,
You'll probably find that Herby's there.

A hibernating Hedgehog,
Woke up to greet the Spring,
He'd set the alarm for half-past May,
But he hadn't heard it ring.
In fact he'd gone and overslept,
A silly thing to do,
Not only had he missed the Spring,
He'd missed the Summer too.

A laughing Hyena named Harry,
Would tell jokes by the score,
At first he was thought to be funny,
But then he became a bore.

He'd crack jokes in the morning,
And then the whole day through,
The other hyenas would laugh a lot,
Because that's what hyenas do.

"If only we could stop laughing,"
They said to themselves one day,
"He'd see that he's not so funny,
And with luck might go away."

Behind Harry's back they practised,
At trying to keep a straight face,
And the next time he started joke-telling,
There wasn't a smile in the place.

Puzzled by their silence,
Harry stopped to wonder why,
He felt a bit embarrassed,
And then began to cry.

At which the other hyenas,
could contain themselves no more,
They laughed until their sides ached,
They were rolling round the floor.

"You horrible things!" Harry cried,
"To make fun of my distress,"
But he never told another joke,
So their scheme worked nonetheless.

If you see a lot of Insects,
   That scurry to and fro,
Please try not to tread on them,
   It's a nasty way to go.

They should appoint a special one,
   To keep them all in line,
With "STOP! INSECTS CROSSING",
   Written on a sign.

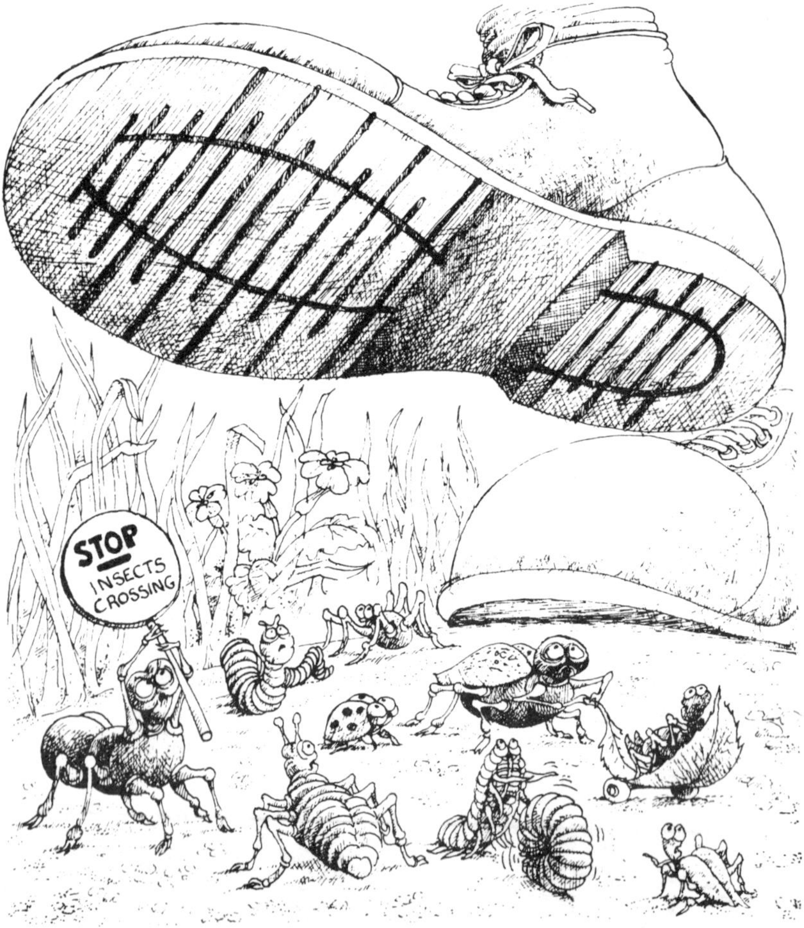

Down in the sea
By the barrier reef,
Is a great big Jellyfish,
Whose name is Keith.
When he moves about,
So big is he,
Enormous waves,
Form on the sea.

And when he laughs,
The sailors curse,
For he shakes and wobbles,
Which makes it worse.
The best thing to do,
Or so I've read,
Is not to sail
Till Keith's in bed.

Kevin was a Kangaroo,
Who dearly loved his mother,
He used to sit inside her pouch,
Along with Bruce, his brother.

But mother took such giant hops,
To get from place to place,
That many times the little lads,
Were thrown out on their face.

They went to see their grandad,
To find out what to do.
He could always sort out problems,
Such a clever Kangaroo.

Grandad got some seat belts,
From an old car on the dump,
And fitted them in mother's pouch,
When she landed from a jump.

So then there was no problem,
For when mother leapt around,
The boys were strapped inside her pouch,
All nicely safe and sound.

Four big Leopards sat up a tree,
One fell out and that left three.
"Climb back up," the three all cried,
Alas he couldn't, for he'd just died.

Murphy hated digging,
He was the laziest of moles,
So he bought himself a big machine
That dug all sorts of holes.
But when it was delivered,
He couldn't make it run,
Despite pressing all the buttons,
It just sat there in the sun.
He found a little lever
And pulled it with a jerk,
The machine started moving
And then it went berserk.
It dug one hole after another,
Great craters in the ground.
"What a mess!" cried Murphy,
As the digger raced around.
He tried in vain to stop it,
But the machine just carried on,
Though finally it did stop,
When all its fuel had gone.
Then a rabbit came to Murphy,
Pulling papers from his hat.
"Council orders," he shouted.
"You can't dig holes like that!"
"You'll have to fill them in at once,"
But Murphy looked at him in pain
And jumped down from the digger.
"I'm not driving that again."
"I don't care," the rabbit said.
"Just do it, it's the law."
So Murphy toiled for years and years
To fill them in by paw.

Nora the Newt lives under a stone,
　　She's awfully timid and shy,
The only time she ever comes out,
　　Is to catch the occasional fly.

She wishes that she could be fierce and bold,
　　Her ancestors were, you know,
Her ancestors being the dinosaurs,
　　That lived millions of years ago.

So if you see Nora it would be nice,
　　To pretend to be frightened and run.
It might increase her confidence,
　　So she'd spend more time in the sun.

Oswald the Ostrich,
  Wished that he could fly,
To be like all the other birds,
  Up there in the sky.

He often practised taking off,
  By running round and round,
And wildly flapping both his wings,
  But he never left the ground.

So Oswald bought some special wings,
  That fixed with a rubber band,
He took off from the highest hill,
  And buried himself in the sand.

Mrs Pig,
Was not very big,
Her husband even smaller,
From morning till evening,
They'd hang from the ceiling,
In the hope that they'd make themselves taller.

The Quail is a quiet bird,
  And never says a lot.
It creeps about along the ground,
  And hopes it won't get shot.

I saw a family of them once,
  At the seaside for the day,
But when I went to say hello,
  They got up and ran away.

Nobody loves a Rat,
They live in dark places,
With long, pointed faces,
Nobody loves a Rat.

Nobody loves a Rat,
They've teeth sharp as nails,
And nasty pink tails,
Nobody loves a Rat.

Nobody loves a Rat,
They're sneaky and mean,
And not very clean,
Nobody loves a Rat.

Nobody loves a Rat,
They bite chickens' legs,
And steal their eggs,
Nobody loves a Rat.

Nobody loves a Rat,
And that's that.

It's awkward being a Rhino,
You can't bend your legs a lot,
I may be many other things,
But agile I am not.

Touching toes is just a joke,
I can barely reach my knees,
And you see, I have a problem,
I cannot scratch my fleas.

Which is why I have a daily help,
A bird called Mrs Hicks,
She really is a treasure,
she eats all my fleas and ticks.

I'm a nasty, horrible shark,
I'll eat anything just for a lark.

They call me the dustbin of the deep,
I eat non-stop as I never sleep.

I chew up people who swim in the sea,
Tin cans, old boots, it's all food to me.

I've even been known to eat billygoats,
And the mucky rubbish that comes from boats.

I'll eat rotten fruit and plastic cups,
I once ate a seal and her five young pups.

I'd have more sense if I had more brains,
Because I always finish with stomach pains,

It's all right for you, you can take pills,
Me, I just have to suffer my ills.

A silly Snail has lost her shell,
She doesn't quite know where,
She had it on an hour before,
And now it isn't there.

Now she's found another one,
Though it doesn't look quite right,
But at least it stops her getting wet,
And is a place to sleep at night.

If you like to sniff at rotten eggs
And decomposing meat,
If you delight in the aroma
Of people's dirty feet,
If you like the smell of mouldy cheese
Wafting round your head,
Then get rid of any pets you have
And get a skunk instead.

"Oh dear," said Mrs. Thrush,
"I've come home in such a rush,
That I quite forgot to get some worms for tea."

"Don't worry dear," said husband Bill,
"I think the shop is open still,
I'll fly down there right now to go and see."

He got there just before
The Wormgrocer closed the door,
Bought some worms and flew back quickly to the tree.

But his journey was for nought,
For it was frozen worms he'd bought,
And they didn't thaw until next day at three.

The Umbrella bird is known to live
  In Ecuador and Peru,
With several aunts and uncles
  In Brazil and Chile too.

It often rains in those parts,
  Which suits them without doubt,
For unless it's raining quite a lot
  Umbrella birds won't come out.

Vulture Vic,
Was feeling sick,
He'd had nothing to eat all week,
Except for a rat,
That was squashed quite flat,
By an elephant down at the creek.

''I must find to eat,
A large lump of meat,
Preferably mouldy and green.''
He searched all around,
But there was none to be found,
Not even a bone could be seen.

Now Vic was so weak,
He could hardly speak,
''I must eat something today.''
As a last resort,
He went and bought
A Chinese take-away.

They call me a grumpy Walrus,
For what reason I cannot see,
Just because I complain a bit,
About things that don't please me.

I'll admit that in the morning,
My patience tends to snap,
And I'm angry in the afternoon,
If I haven't had my nap.

I know that noisy youngsters,
Who come a bit too near,
Make me lose my temper,
And I box them on the ear.

"Just relax and take a dip,"
Is what I'm always being told,
And that just makes me raging mad,
Because the water's freezing cold.

"Why am I so ugly?"
Sighed Wanda to herself,
"No-one wants to marry me,
And I'm left upon the shelf.
I know I'm only a Warthog
And uglier than most,
But I'm very good at sewing,
And I never burn the toast.
My hair is always combed,
My tusks are always sharp,
I can sing the latest pop songs,
And play upon the harp.
I was only once proposed to,
Back in Nineteen Sixty-Three,
But the reason I turned him down,
Was that he was uglier than me."

Willy the Worm was very very long,
A very long worm was he;
If he turned his head he could see his back,
Just as far as his eye could see.

He never got a good night's sleep,
No matter how he tried,
For if one half lay upon the bed,
The other hung over the side.

Only on very long trips indeed
Could Willy's tail be seen.
He'd pass it on the way back home
Going where his front had been.

But he didn't really mind his length,
There was one good thing he found,
Birds got so tired of eating him
They'd drop him on the ground.

You don't have to ask the X-ray fish,
  What it's had for dinner or tea,
Because the X-ray fish is transparent,
  So you just have to look and see.

Though I've never actually seen one,
  I'm told worms are its favourite dish,
Which only shows it's much the same,
  As any other old fish.

A Yak is very hairy,
Which keeps him nice and warm,
It also keeps him dry inside,
If he goes out in a storm.

But as a Yak gets older,
He goes bald upon his head,
So it won't be real hair you see,
But a false hair-piece instead.

Before a Zebra goes to bed,
He slides his stripes off over his head,
Then lays them out upon the ground,
And covers them up with grass he's found.
He sleeps on top of the stripes and grass,
Until the morning comes to pass,
Then up he gets and soon is dressed
In a set of stripes all nicely pressed.